GAYLE
FORMAN

GAYLE FORMAN

SUSAN MEYER

ROSEN PUBLISHING®

New York

Published in 2016 by The Rosen Publishing Group, Inc.
29 East 21st Street, New York, NY 10010

Copyright © 2016 by The Rosen Publishing Group, Inc.

First Edition

Library of Congress Cataloging-in-Publication Data

Meyer, Susan, 1986-
  Gayle Forman / Susan Meyer. — First edition.
    pages cm. — (All about the author)
  Includes bibliographical references and index.
  ISBN 978-1-4994-6272-2 (library bound)
  1. Forman, Gayle—Juvenile literature. 2. Authors,
American—21st century—Biography—Juvenile literature.
3. Young adult fiction—Authorship—Juvenile literature. I.
Title.
  PS3613.E74773Z75 2016
  813'.6—dc23
  [B]
                                          2015020200

Manufactured in China

CONTENTS

Making choices is a big part of growing up. Sometimes you make choices in life, and sometimes choices make you." This quote comes from the novel *If I Stay* by the young adult author Gayle Forman. Forman's writing has enchanted millions of people of all ages around the world. Forman has published many best-selling novels. *If I Stay* alone had sold more than 2.4 million copies internationally as of 2014, according to *Publishers Weekly*.

Just as the quote says, life is a mix of luck, choices, and decisions forced by circumstances. Gayle Forman's life story is no different. Her successes are a product of great talent, but also many choices have led her to where she is today. Her path to young adult fiction was not a direct one. It was a combination of hard work and following where her choices took her that led Forman to her achievements. As a writer and a citizen of the world, she has worn many hats throughout her life: daughter, traveler, magazine writer, journalist, wife, mother, best-selling author, and even Bollywood film extra.

She is a lover of travel and of cultivating new experiences and new friendships. She enjoys collecting people's stories, which in turn can inspire the stories she writes. Before going to college, she traveled the world and took odd jobs while she figured out what she wanted to do. She briefly considered

Gayle Forman, seen here at a book signing, didn't become a best-selling novelist overnight. In fact, she didn't write her first novel until she was 34.

being a doctor, but after chancing on a journalism class (by following a cute boy), she discovered she loved to write and tell people's stories. She worked as a journalist for *Seventeen* magazine and published a travel memoir before she turned her focus to fiction. Not only fiction, but young adult fiction, as that was the audience she felt she connected with the best. She admires her many fans for their intelligence and ability to connect with characters. She thinks many people don't give enough credit to teenagers and to young adult fiction.

Her first novel, *Sisters in Sanity*, was not an immediate success. However, her second novel, *If I Stay*, was a smash hit. The 2009 book was made into a movie, which grossed over $78 million worldwide, in 2014. She wrote a follow-up to the book called *Where She Went*. She has also published several other novels and an e-book novella. Forman

Gayle Forman (*center*) poses with Chloë Grace Moretz and Jamie Blackley, who played the characters Mia and Adam in the film adaptation of Forman's beloved *If I Stay*.

continues to write from her home in Brooklyn, where she lives with her husband and two daughters.

Forman is an incisive writer and powerful storyteller. She has listened to and heard stories from people all over the world. She seeks inspiration everywhere and compiles it all into a rich tapestry of storytelling. She had the good fortune to be born to parents who encouraged her love of travel and independence at an early age. They also gave her the courage to explore and always be curious about the world. She has a gift for making friends and learning about people wherever she goes and for celebrating what makes people unique. She considers herself a misfit who gets along best with other people who are doing what they love without concern for what the rest of the world thinks. Ultimately, all of her experiences add to her writing to make it stronger and more relatable.

A CALIFORNIA DREAMER

Gayle Forman would one day come to write the stories of many men and women both real and fictional. Her own story began on June 5, 1970, when she was born in Los Angeles, California. Her parents were Ruth and Lee Forman. Forman describes her parents as very antimaterialistic. They instilled in her the value of experiences over possessions. An older sister and a brother rounded out the Forman clan.

A FREETHINKING FAMILY

Forman and her siblings were raised Jewish, and she continues to practice the religion to this day. Forman has said on her blog that her family believed strongly in family values like expressing

love unconditionally and doing volunteer work to help the community. That said, certain other traditional family values were considered less important. For example, salty language wasn't considered a problem in the Forman household. To this day, Forman is surprised by the outrage and offense that the profanity used by characters in her books causes.

The Formans weren't the everyday American family. Ruth and Lee took their children on backpacking trips across Europe, to peace marches, and on hiking trips. They wanted their children to learn about the world through these experiences. Early upbringing plays no small part in later interests. Forman would discover a lifelong love of travel. This wanderlust would become a driving force in her life. She would spend the first few decades of her life exploring and seeking out new people and places.

The area around Los Angeles, California, is full of hiking opportunities. The Forman family traveled far and wide, but they also had plenty of adventures right in their own backyard.

Because of her freethinking parents, Forman did not have the typical childhood. She was taught to value individuality. She seldom strived to do anything just because other people were doing it or felt the need to fit in. While other children might have wished to be firefighters or doctors, her earliest career aspiration was to be the sun. (As she says on her official website, she was later disappointed to find out this was not a realizable job prospect.) Even knowing that becoming the sun wasn't an option, she never really considered being a writer. As she said in an interview in the *Guardian,* "I wasn't one of those kids who grew up wanting to write or who read a particular book and thought: 'I want to do that!' I always told stories and wrote them down, but I never thought writing was a career path." What she didn't know then was that behind every good writer there is first and foremost a storyteller. The same qualities that made her love to explore and be curious about new things also happen to be the makings of a budding writer.

NEVER FITTING IN

Forman liked being different and enjoyed the independence her parents had encouraged in her. Unfortunately, her inability to fit in led to some teasing from the other girls at her small Jewish elementary school. They made fun of the clothes she wore and the music she listened to. It didn't faze Forman too much. She didn't see the point in listening to Kenny Loggins when what she really liked was punk, just to follow along with her peers. As luck would have it, while elementary school did not provide many lifelong friendships, Forman would soon find her tribe.

One summer when Forman was in middle school, her mother enrolled her in a theater camp outside Los Angeles in the San Fernando Valley. The camp was a perfect incubator for artistic-minded kids who didn't care what anyone else thought about them. During her summer at the camp, Forman transformed from a quiet girl trying to figure out her place in the world to a talkative adolescent happy to have discovered open-minded friends. In her travel memoir, *You Can't Get There From Here*, Forman describes herself in this period of her life as "spastic" and something of a "motor-mouth."

While the camp didn't transform her into a lifelong thespian, it did help her to find some wonderful friends. Now that she knew there were people out in the world who would understand her, she just needed to go forth and find them. In

As both an aspiring actress and an aspiring redhead, Forman was a huge fan of teen star Molly Ringwald. The author said she used to bite her lip like Ringwald did and now has a permanent scar.

middle school and high school, the transformation continued. Far from being shy, she couldn't wait to get out into the world to find more people to talk to and more new places to discover.

ACROSS THE POND

Through elementary school and middle school, Forman was able to travel a great deal with her family on vacations. However, it was when she was still in high school that Forman would set out on her first international travels alone.

Forman received her first taste of living abroad when she was only sixteen. She studied as an exchange student in England. She lived with a host family outside of Leicester. This is a small town in the East Midlands of England that is best known as the burial place of Richard III. She studied at nearby Countesthorpe College. In addition to being in a foreign country, the school itself wasn't your everyday high school. It had an experimental educational program focused on free thinking rather than on the typical classroom experience. As Forman herself describes it in her book *You Can't Get There From Here:* "If you weren't a hippie, a punk, a vegetarian, or a sworn enemy of capitalism, you were the misfit at this school." Ever sympathizing with the misfits and those who march to the beat of their own drum, Forman felt like she fit right in. In fact, she describes the year she spent at Countesthorpe College as one of the best years of her life. She also said it changed the trajectory of her life. She now realized she didn't have to follow a certain path and continue schooling in a certain way. The world was wide open and waiting.

She returned to the United States after a year abroad in order to finish high school in California, but the travel bug had been planted. After she graduated from high school, she decided not to go to college right away. Instead, she wanted to travel again, this time without a set semester schedule. She told her parents that she would be learning

Leicester, England, seen here, is the closest city to Countesthorpe College. It was there that a teenaged Gayle Forman spent a year studying abroad.

FIVE FAST FACTS ABOUT FORMAN

1. Forman has been to more than sixty countries and has learned (and unfortunately forgotten) three foreign languages.
2. It's no secret that Forman loves travel, and she says if she could have any career other than a writer, it would be a travel agent.
3. In terms of what career she wouldn't want? Forman says her least favorite job was when she worked as a data entry clerk.
4. Forman loves to read but prefers to write. If she were stranded on a desert island and could bring any three books, she would take three blank notebooks to fill with her own words.
5. Her astrological sign is Gemini, which she thinks describes her perfectly: independent and quick tempered.

more from the university of life than by studying at an official institution of higher learning. True to form, Ruth and Lee supported their daughter in following her dreams and making her own choices. And thus, while still a teenager, Forman set out with a one-way ticket to Europe, embarking on the next chapter of her life.

THE UNIVERSITY OF LIFE

F orman didn't have a set plan for the next few years of her life. She wanted to try different jobs, meet new people, and generally just live her life on her own terms. She was young and excited about the world in front of her. She arrived in Europe in the late 1980s. She began traveling with an English friend she had met during her time at Countesthorpe named Rebecca. They didn't stay in England for long but packed up their backpacks and headed out to see the continent of Europe.

LIVING IN EUROPE

Forman traveled around Europe for three years, adding ever more stamps to her passport and new experiences to her life.

During her travels, she made interesting friends, including a troupe of street performers in Italy and drag queens in Denmark. She loved learning about people and was especially drawn to hearing the stories of others embracing life, doing their own thing, and not worrying about fitting into a prescribed mold. She travelled with Rebecca for a while, but the pair parted ways when Forman decided to stop traveling the continent in favor of settling down in Amsterdam. Amsterdam is the capital city of the Netherlands. It is the cultural and economic center of the country and is known for its system of canals and bikeable streets.

Forman lived in Amsterdam for a year and a half. Many years later, she still describes Amsterdam

Amsterdam is a city known for its extensive network of canals. The city is made up of ninety islands connected by four hundred stone bridges and sixty-two miles (one hundred kilometers) of waterways.

as one of her favorite cities in the world, second only to New York, where she lives now. It was in Amsterdam that she first experienced heartbreak after falling in and out of love with a Dutch bartender. This particular character in her life would later show up in her trio of novels *Just One Day, Just One Year,* and *Just One Night.* While living in Amsterdam, Forman worked a number of odd jobs to get by, including stints as a hotel maid at a youth hostel and a flower seller.

Forman is adamant that her early experiences abroad contributed to her later becoming a journalist and young adult writer. As she described in her personal blog: "Living abroad tweaked the way my life was going, opened it up, made things that might seem otherwise impossible seem possible." While her life abroad was exciting and there was always some new adventure around the corner, after a few years, she was ready to return to her home country. She knew what she wanted the next stage of her life to look like and was ready to begin a new phase of her education.

ONWARD TO OREGON

After her time in Amsterdam, Forman was ready to leave the university of life for more formal education back in the United States. Her travels had the intended effect and she now had an idea of what she wanted to do with her life. Naturally, her idea involved further traveling. She planned to become a doctor so she could return to traveling but this time with the purpose of helping people through the organization Doctors Without Borders. This organization sends doctors from the United States to third-world countries that do not often have access to advanced medicine and reliable medical practitioners. The organization was founded in 1971, and today more than thirty thousand doctors and nurses volunteer their time to global health issues.

Doctors Without Borders operates in seventy countries around the globe. Here, a doctor with the organization helps a patient in the city of Kunduz in Afghanistan.

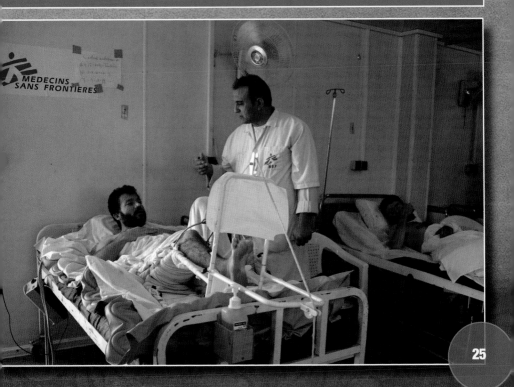

With the aim of getting a premed degree, she enrolled at the University of Oregon in Eugene. Unfortunately, she would soon find out that the study of medicine was not one that came easily to her. She was soon ready to quit. Because she didn't have an idea of what she wanted to do outside of medicine, she nearly dropped out of school altogether. However, while working toward her degree in the sciences, she'd also ended up taking a handful of writing classes. One of them was a journalism class. In a 2009 interview with *Publishers Weekly*, she revealed that she took this particular class only because a boy she had had a crush on was taking it. It was supposed to be a very difficult course that would make or break aspiring journalists. In Forman's case, it made one. This class would remove all thoughts of going prenmed or leaving college without a degree. She had found a new calling. Forman would graduate from the University of Oregon with a degree in journalism in 1996.

A PERFECT MATCH

In addition to embarking on an exciting new career path, Forman would gain something else very important at the University of Oregon: a lifelong travel partner and love. Forman met her husband, Nick Tucker, during her time at school. She describes him

THE OREGON STORY

Gayle Forman's best-selling young adult title *If I Stay* is set in Oregon. So are parts of its sequel, *Where She Went*. Additionally, characters from several of her other novels hail from the Pacific Northwest. Forman had lived all over the world by the time she wrote all of these novels. It is interesting that she chose to set them in Oregon instead of one of the other interesting places she had lived, in the Los Angeles area where she had grown up, or in Brooklyn where she and her family live now.

Forman lived in Oregon from 1991 until 1996. Initially, upon moving to Eugene, she was not taken with it. It was a small town and felt confining to the world traveler who'd grown accustomed to cosmopolitan cities. But she soon discovered a thriving underground music scene and met many good friends, some of whom she has remained friends with to this day. It didn't hurt that she also met her husband, Nick Tucker, in Oregon.

Ultimately, Oregon represented an important turning point in Forman's life. Her decision to set one of her first novels there is proof of the state's important role in her own life. Adam, one of the main characters in *If I Stay*, is in a band in the exploding Oregon music scene, much like Forman's own husband was when she met him. Forman has said that in writing about a young love story set in Oregon, she brought a lot of her own feelings for her husband into the story.

at the time that they met as a blue-haired punk-rock librarian, and one who was as enamored with her weirdness as she was with his. He was in a band, and she was involved in the burgeoning music scene in Eugene at the time. At one point, he and his band asked her to collaborate on a show with them, even though she was not a musician. The two were friends for over a year before they started dating.

After college, Forman and her husband would leave Oregon together and travel across the country to New York City, where they would settle in Brooklyn. Neither was particularly traditional, but after six years of dating, they decided to get married. As Forman had come

Gayle Forman says her husband, Nick, helped inspire the character of Adam in *If I Stay*. Here, he supports his wife at the premiere of the movie adaptation of that book.

to realize, he had become her family. Naturally, for these two nonconformists, their wedding was an edgy punk rock Jewish ceremony. One of Nick's ex-girlfriends even officiated.

With a partner to continue her life's travels with, and having left Oregon and the university life behind, Forman was ready to start her career in earnest. It might not have been her childhood aspiration, but somewhere along the way she had become a writer. Now that she was in New York—a hotbed for publishing, journalism, and art—she had the opportunity to prove it.

STATESIDE SUCCESS

On arriving in New York and settling down in Brooklyn with Nick, Forman had a very specific goal in mind. Since becoming a journalist and writer, she had dreamed of working at the punk and indie rock teen magazine *Sassy*. The magazine was founded in 1988 by an Australian feminist named Sandra Yates. Its focus on music and individuality made it exactly the publication Forman wanted to work for. Unfortunately, the magazine had stopped publishing in 1996, before Forman even arrived in the city. She needed a backup plan.

Instead of *Sassy*, she was able to get a job working for another well-known teen publication: *Seventeen*. Started in

Seventeen has changed a lot since its earliest issues in the 1940s. Today, the publication reaches over two million readers and offers fashion tips, celebrity news, and stories from real teens.

1944, the publication was the first magazine published in the United States expressly for a teen audience. While the magazine is often thought of in terms of its fashion and beauty focus, its original intent was to inspire teen girls to become responsible citizens. Forman says friends were always surprised that she was able to write a number of hard-hitting journalistic articles during her time there.

TURNING *SEVENTEEN*

Forman quickly took to her job at *Seventeen*. She loved writing, and she especially loved the magazine's audience of teenage girls. She felt that many people don't give teenagers enough credit. They think that teens are apathetic and uninterested in world issues. She happily discovered that her audience loved to read about serious issues and had a great capacity for empathy. She could write about teen girls in a refugee camp on the other side of the world and her audience would understand the issues at stake and want to help the people in the article. She also enjoyed how engaged her audience was. As she described in an interview in the *Guardian*, "[Teens] will respond passionately to an article they like and if they hate

"GIRLS IN EXILE"

While many associate *Seventeen* with fashion ads and light journalism, the magazine does include pieces designed to help illuminate the world for its readers. Gayle Forman wrote such articles during her time at the magazine. She valued her audience and knew that young women could and would care about important global issues.

In a 2001 article, "Girls in Exile," she wrote about four young women who were refugees in Afghanistan. The introduction for the article could be the start of a novel if it weren't tragically a true story:

> *What if you had to run from the home you knew or lie to the people you love just so you could go to school? Meet four Afghan refugee girls fighting for their right to be educated.*

What made Forman's nonfiction essays so compelling is that she sought the human stories at the root of larger issues. She knew her teen audience would want to know about serious issues affecting other teens both nearby and around the globe.

it they'll let you know." This openness and free criticism was just the sort of accountability the young Forman was looking for as she honed her journalistic chops.

She soon discovered she had a talent for reaching the demographic. She has joked in interviews that it is because she herself still has the mind of a teenage girl. She had a knack for writing compelling stories that were accessible and never patronizing. Over time, she became *Seventeen*'s senior writer. During her time at the magazine, she wrote about issues ranging from child soldiers in Sierra Leone and unrest in Northern Ireland to migrant workers in the United States. Many of her articles focused on issues of social justice.

NONFICTION AND FICTION

While she showed great talent writing for a teen audience, Forman also pursued freelance writing opportunities at a number of other publications, including *Jane, Cosmopolitan,* and the *Nation.* Her writing for *Jane* magazine was a nice nod to her original dream of writing for *Sassy*, as the creator of *Jane*, Jane Pratt, was also the original editor of *Sassy*. For all her publications, Forman's

Jane Pratt is the founding editor of both *Sassy* and *Jane* magazines. Like Forman, she has made a career of publishing content for young women. In an interview with the *New York Times*, she said that writing for that audience will never get old.

writing was mostly long-form journalistic pieces. Happily some of her journalistic pursuits, both at *Seventeen* and elsewhere, also involved travel, so she was able to continue to embrace her love of travel.

Forman explains in interviews that telling other people's stories is what taught her narrative form. She had not intended to become a writer of fiction but developed the skill over time through her nonfiction writing. In nonfiction it is important to cite facts and verify sources, while in fiction imagination can take over. Initially the two crafts might seem very different. However, in writing long-form journalism pieces, the structure and dialogue is similar. Learning to tell people's stories in a way that grips the audience and makes them care is a necessity, whether you are writing about real people or creating characters out of thin air. Forman described the similarities between fiction and nonfiction in a 2014 interview with the Vancouver news outlet *Permanent Rain Press*, explaining that both fiction and nonfiction have their difficulties. She said, "There's a different standard of truth when you're writing fiction… but it has to ring true, even if it's completely made up."

Switching to writing fiction after writing nonfiction can be a big leap. Fiction writing is a whole other ball game. In interviews, Forman has described the switch from fiction to nonfiction for her as both a big change and also a gradual change. She had no idea she would one day come to write fiction until one of the ideas in her head demanded to be written. Before she could begin to write fiction, she had one more very long journey to make. It would be her most extensive travel yet and also lead to the creation of her first book.

WHERE SHE WENT

Forman is both adventurous and independent, and many of her travel adventures were undertaken alone, although she always made new friends and travel companions along the way. However, in 2001, she set off on a trip different from all her previous ones. This time it was a planned year-long voyage around the world with her husband, Nick. She said many people assumed the trip was her idea because of her globe-trotting past. But it was actually Nick who wanted to see the world, as he was tired of taking trips for just a few weeks when he could get time off from work. Although she was getting some traction in her journalism career, Forman couldn't say no to a year of travel with her love. She decided to put her journalism career on hold to join him and travel for one year. She also decided to write about the journey. Her hope was that, in addition to enjoying the trip, she could also try out a different medium from nonfiction articles. She was ready to write her first book.

The couple planned to depart in late 2001, but their itinerary was somewhat altered with the terrorist attacks on the World Trade Center on September 11, 2001. At this time, relations were shaky between the United States and some countries in the Middle East. It wouldn't be as safe for Americans to travel in this region. The pair decided to avoid the Middle East during their travels because of the shaky political climate and tense relations with the United States. That still left much of the world to explore, and the couple made it to four continents during their yearlong adventure.

POLYNESIA TO ASIA

One of Forman's requirements for the trip was that they begin it at the beach. Thus, they started the trip in Tonga, a remote Polynesian island chain in the South Pacific. There Forman sought out and befriended a group of people called the *fakaleiti*. The *fakaleiti* are Tongans who are born biologically male but act and dress in a way that is female. Culturally

Forman enjoyed meeting and learning about the *fakaleiti* while researching the complicated politics of gender in Tonga. Here a *fakaleiti* singer performs at a bar in Tonga.

in Tonga they are treated as a third gender, neither male nor female. When she described this portion of the trip, Forman wrote in depth about her friendships with the *fakaleiti* and the delicate place they hold in Tongan society. From Tonga, after a brief stopover in quiet New Zealand, Forman and her husband moved on to China.

China is the most populous country in the world, with over a billion people living there. It has experienced a rapid change in the last two decades and is home to factories that produce many of the items used in the United States. As China has entered the global market and economy, the demand for English teachers and people who speak English increased dramatically there. This was the China that Forman

More than 170 individual islands make up the Polynesian nation of Tonga. Many of these islands are uninhabited and lined with white sand beaches and tropical rainforests.

and Nick arrived to in the early 2000s.

In China, the pair settled themselves in the capital city of Beijing, where Forman made friends with—or rather became the somewhat unwilling editor of—a Chinese doctor writing a book about English. After meeting him by chance, he latched on and badgered her with early-morning phone calls, insisting she edit his manuscript. Even though her essays about the trip are nonfiction, the characters like this Chinese doctor, who she refers to as Doctor Bi, really come alive on the page. And unlike much of her later fiction writing, her nonfiction travel writing is full of lighthearted humor. While she expresses some exasperation about her time with Dr. Bi, she is at least able to weave a good story out of it.

From China, the pair traveled south to Thailand. Thailand is a small but beautiful country on Asia's Indochinese peninsula. In 2001, when Forman visited it, Thailand's population was around sixty-two million people. Unfortunately, there is a great divide between rich and poor people in Thailand. Poor children often beg on the streets for money and food, especially in areas where tourism is popular. While in Thailand, Forman learned a lot from talking to Thai street children. She describes the overwhelming feeling of helplessness that comes from being surrounded by extreme poverty. Some of the street kids she talked to are rather remarkable and speak snippets of many languages in order to engage tourists, because their livelihood

Street children, like this girl in northern Thailand, were a common, but disturbing, site for Forman. A U.S. State Department report estimated that there are twenty thousand children living on the streets in Thailand's cities.

and survival depends on selling trinkets to visiting foreigners. Forman had often written about issues of social justice affecting young people while working at *Seventeen*, so focusing on children and teens in poverty while in Thailand was a natural fit for her.

After Thailand, she and Nick traveled through Cambodia. They thought of going to Yemen in the Middle East afterward, but with the political situation still fraught, they decided to skip it. That made their next stop India, where Forman achieved her dream, or at least satisfied her curiosity, of finding out what it was like to be an extra in a Bollywood film. When she and Nick were watching a Bollywood film, she'd noticed that there were many white extras populating the background. She wondered where they had all come from. Her curiosity got the better of her and she decided to wander ar Mumbai to see if she could get cast. It wasn't long before she was! She enjoyed the experien although she did not decide to become a frequ extra as many expats and tourists did. Deman high, but she had other plans and places to ex ence. Interestingly, years later, she would appe an extra in the movie version of her own book

rjun Rampal, seen here at an event in 2006, is a famous Bollywood actor. He starred in the movie *Humko Tumse Pyaar Hai*, in which Forman made her Bollywood debut as an extra.

Stay. She says she would be surprised if anyone can spot her in *If I Stay*, but she is a person in the hospital waiting room.

A BOLLYWOOD DREAM

Being in a movie usually takes a little special training. Even being an extra in a movie can be hard to do. For Gayle Forman, it was about being in the right place at the right time. Well, sort of.

Forman had heard that Bollywood movies were constantly looking for white people to be in the background of films. Bollywood is the Indian film industry based in Mumbai. The word comes from the "B" in Bombay (another name for Mumbai) and Hollywood, the center of the American film industry. Hundreds of Bollywood films are released each year. Bollywood films have a distinctive style. They are often escapist fantasies with elaborate costumes, scenery, and dance numbers.

Bollywood movies, especially those set in the United States, often feature white extras in the background as waiters, partygoers, and pedestrians. Forman was scouted, dressed up in a bright blue gown, and paid $10 a day to stand in the back of a dance scene. Eventually the luster wore off the thrill of being in a movie and she left the business, but not without a story to tell.

Big dance numbers feature in many Bollywood films. These women are performing a dance routine for the opening of a Bollywood movie at a movie theater in Madrid, Spain.

Following her brush with stardom in India, Forman and Nick moved on to Kazakhstan. Kazakhstan is a country in central Asia. It used to be part of the Soviet Union but became independent in the early 1990s. While in Kazakhstan, Forman spent much of her time learning about a

RUSSIA

opavl

Pavlodar.

●ASTANA

Semey   Oskemen   MONG.

Karaganda●

TAN

Lake Balkhash

orda

.Almaty   CHINA

Taraz
nkent   KYRGYZSTAN

Kazakhstan is a country in Central Asia. It is south of Russia and northwest of China. It
covers 1,052,090 square miles (2,724,900 sq km), making it about four times the size of
Texas.

group of Tolkienists. This group of Kazak young
folk was obsessed with the Lord of the Rings
books written by J. R. R. Tolkien. The group would

The Lord of the Rings series by J. R. R. Tolkien has captured the hearts and minds of people around the globe, not just in Kazakhstan. More than 150 million copies of the books have been sold.

perform elaborate reenactments where everyone would dress up as elves and hobbits and act in elaborate battles. Forman was able to journey into the hills and attend one of these events. In some cases, Forman would discover the kids and teens had not actually read the books but just enjoyed the spectacle and costuming. She didn't know it yet, but Forman, too, would come to write novels that excited a large teen fan base, albeit one without quite so much pageantry.

AFRICA TO EUROPE

After her time with the youth of Kazakhstan, Forman and her husband were ready to leave Asia. The pair continued the journey to the continent of Africa. The first stop was Tanzania, a small nation in East Africa known for its vast plains and wildlife. Additionally, Tanzania

While Forman was fascinated by Tanzania's music scene, the majority of the tourists who visit the country do so for its wildlife. These zebras and wildebeests are grazing in the country's Ngorongoro Conservation Area.

has a strong rap and hip-hop scene dating back to the 1980s when Tanzanian youth were inspired by the hip-hop music in the United States. Even though she never played an instrument, other than dabbling in guitar, music has always been an important part of Forman's life. It features heavily in many of her novels. While in Tanzania, she befriended several Tanzanian rappers and musicians. She also wrote about some of the issues they face, including often not seeing the bulk of the money made from their shows.

After Tanzania, Forman traveled to the country of South Africa. The nation had recently experienced a major shift in 1994 when a period of systematic racial segregation called apartheid ended, making the country a democracy. Forman did not choose to focus on the interesting political climate left in the wake of apartheid. Instead she had a very specific reason for being in South Africa. As you may remember, Forman practices Judaism. She had read that she might be able to connect with her Jewish heritage in a surprising place: around South Africa and Zimbabwe. There she was able to meet members of an ethnic group called the Lemba. Lemba tradition claims that the group has Jewish ancestry. There are some striking similarities between Lemba practice and Jewish customs, though the Lemba's lives are quite different from those of Jews of the Western world. Scientific studies and DNA tests have provided some veracity to their claims of ancestry. At the time that

This leader of the Lemba people, at a meeting in Harare, Zimbabwe, is telling the story of the group's background and how the lost tribe of Israel arrived in Africa.

Forman was in South Africa, there were approximately fifty thousand Lemba in existence. Forman was fascinated by the Lemba and interviewed many about their experiences and customs. She was interested to see the ways in which their understanding of what it means to be Jewish was different from her own.

After exploring Africa, Forman and her husband ended their trip in Forman's old stomping grounds in Europe. The focus of the end of their trip was on Amsterdam, where Forman had lived a decade prior. She enjoyed being able to show her husband her favorite haunts. Living in and traveling around Europe had an important impact on her life, and she wanted to share that. Long after this trip to Amsterdam, a plot line about a girl traveling to Europe for the first time would later form the basis of her book *Just One Day.*

Throughout their year of traveling, Forman had chronicled stories from the young and old and from all walks of life. She once said that one of the reasons she enjoyed being a journalist was that it gave her a professional reason for butting into other people's business. The truth is, nosiness and curiosity about the world are two great assets for any storyteller.

GETTING PUBLISHED

Forman wrote all about her year of traveling. The people that she met and their stories were the focus. The resulting book would become her first full-length published manuscript. The book's full published title was *You Can't Get There From Here: A Year on the Fringes of a Shrinking World*. It was not your typical travel memoir. It was divided into eight main essays set in eight of the places she visited. Each essay talks about a specific, and often fascinating, point of the culture there. Forman has always said that she is the type to skip major tourist attractions when traveling and instead seek out the most interesting aspect of a place off the beaten track. The one thing all the essays in the book have in common is that they all focus on the people of a place. And it would be fair to say, many of the essays focus on the misfits and outsiders of a place. For example, Tolkienists are a small minority in Kazakhstan and there are not very many members of the Lemba.

It is not always easy to get published for the first time. Forman describes the process of getting her first publishing contract as a wild ride. She had to write a book proposal and some sample chapters of the book. A book proposal is submitted by an author to get publishers enthusiastic about the book and tell them what it will be about. She was so excited

Forman's "Team Adam" T-shirt is a reference to the hero in *If I Stay*. Forman says that being "Team Adam" means being "on the side of guys who act like men, and men who treat girls and women with respect."

when multiple editors and publishing houses were interested in publishing her book. Then several of the editors dropped out of the running. She learned early in her book publishing career that rejection and disappointment are a big part of the writing game. Luckily, after all was said and done, two publishers were still interested. She was happy to see the fruits of her labor in print for the first time. However, the book publishing process was also a learning experience for her. Of all her books, *You Can't Get There From Here* is the only one whose title she didn't choose, and incidentally the only one whose title she hates. The book arrived but was not the hit Forman had hoped. What she didn't know was that several best sellers were just around the corner. And more surprisingly still, they would be fiction.

Some changes in Forman's personal life would soon necessitate changes in the type of writing Forman would look to do. As luck would have it, she would soon discover she was more successful at fiction than nonfiction.

FIVE

CHAPTER

PUBLISHING PAGE-TURNERS

G ayle Forman's first publishing contract, for *You Can't Get There From Here*, had led to a successfully published book. This book, along with her previous journalism pursuits, enabled her to combine two things she loved: writing and travel. But her life would soon change in a big way. First, her daughter Willa was born. Later she and Nick adopted their daughter Denbelle. Now, as much as she loved travel, she had found something she loved more that kept her close to home. She no longer wanted to take writing assignments that would take her away from her family. However, there were still bills to pay so she knew she needed to continue writing. Born out of this necessity, she decided to try writing not from her travels but from her imagination.

Her life experiences, and the stories she collected from all the people she met, had made her an ideal storyteller.

Forman likes to stay connected to her audience. She regularly blogs and posts updates about her work. She also sometimes makes school visits and does readings to promote her newest books.

Choosing to write for a young adult audience on her first foray into fiction was a natural choice. She had loved writing for teens and young women early in her career. It was a tone and style that came more easily to her. She describes herself as feeling like she's still a teenager. In a 2009 interview with *Publishers Weekly,* she described beginning to write young adult fiction as "coming full circle" in her career and finally "coming home."

HER FIRST NOVEL

In 2007, her first young adult novel would be published. It was called *Sisters in Sanity.* The novel was actually based on an article she had written on true events back when she worked for *Seventeen*. As she first dipped her feet in the fiction pool, she had a factual backstory to fall back on. She had previously toyed with the idea of writing a nonfiction piece about the subject of adolescent boot camps. When she set down to write it, however, it would become her first novel. *Sisters in Sanity* tells the story of Brit Hemphill, who is committed by her family to a supposed treatment center for wayward teens that is actually a sham. She bonds with some of the girls at the center but has trouble knowing whom she can trust.

Once Forman started to write the book, the words just poured out of her. In the first weekend she started to write *Sisters in Sanity,* she wrote twelve thousand words. That is more than the length of this biography! Because Forman had been thinking about the idea for so long and had already done research about the camps and situations she was writing about, the actual writing happened at a frenzied pace.

Sisters in Sanity would not have the initial commercial success of her later books. The publishing house didn't promote it very much and the release bombed. Around the same time, Forman found herself, because of circumstances beyond her control, without an agent, a publishing house, or an editor. In some ways, even though she had a major success in having her first novel published, she felt like she was returning to the beginning of her career. She describes the response to *Sisters in Sanity* as a turning point in her career. She knew there were only so many failed novels she could have before publishing companies would stop being willing to take a chance on her. She had to choose not to let these feelings of failure get her down. Instead, she chose to keep writing and to nourish a little story that had been growing in her head.

Mia being a cellist was one of Forman's earliest inspirations about the character. Forman had to research how to play the cello in order to make the character believable.

IF I STAY

In an interview for the blog *First Novels Club*, Forman described the process of writing what would become her best-selling novel. For years it was just an idea that she couldn't get out of her head. It was a question that haunted her. If your family were lost and you were hovering between life and death…what if you could choose whether you lived or died? Forman said the character of Mia came to her fully formed as a cellist. Forman herself was not a classically trained musician, so she had to do a lot of research to make the character and her passion believable. However, she does enjoy the cello, believing it to be an almost human sounding instrument.

What Forman didn't find difficult was capturing the teenage voice. Some critics thought that Mia sounded too mature for her sixteen years, but to Forman she was just precocious enough. Forman said she purposely didn't research teenage slang, but instead wrote to a teenage point of view, something she was comfortable with given her writing background. Much like her writing for *Seventeen*, Forman didn't want to talk down to her audience. She wanted to provide her readers with characters who were every bit as complex and language that was as interesting as that in novels targeted at adults.

Even though fiction is a creative experience, it does usually take some research. Forman writes realistic fiction. Instead of fantasy or science fiction, her stories take place in our world in the present time. For this reason, she has to make sure her books sound logical and make sense. For example, in *If I Stay*, some of the action takes place in hospital emergency rooms. To make the action realistic, Forman had to learn the language to make her doctor's dialogue and actions sound real. Luckily, while Forman herself never became a doctor, she had a friend who worked in an emergency room who could give her an inside look.

Another important aspect of the novel is the music. In addition to the classical music important to Mia's identity as a devoted cellist, Forman incorporated a lot of rock music into her story. As Forman described in an interview, the music added texture to the novel and made the tragic parts easier to handle. The soundtrack for the book includes punk rock and classic old school rock from the Ramones to the Smiths. Music was always an important part of Forman's life and one of the main reasons she set the book in Oregon. After all, the

The English rock band the Smiths is seen here playing a concert in 1984. In *If I Stay*, Forman incorporates music from the Smiths as well as songs by Alice Cooper, Frank Sinatra, Bob Marley, and many others.

music scene there in the early 1990s had been an important influence on her.

The plot of *If I Stay* hinges on the choice that Mia must make: whether to live or to die. Forman said she didn't know the ending until halfway through the book. She could see a legitimate argument to each choice. Because of the subject matter, the book is tragic. Forman has said that all of the parts that are sad to read were also very sad for her to write. She was emotionally tied to her characters and their struggles.

When the book came out, it was soon clear it would be a much greater success than *Sisters in Sanity*. Writing a book that skyrockets to the top of best seller lists is exciting for any author, but it was especially so for Forman, who knew what it was like to have a book bomb. She wasn't able to sleep every night as she nervously watched the reviews come in. The book soon spread around the world, selling more than two million copies. In the United Kingdom, a young adult and an adult version were released. In 2014, a movie version would follow that shot the book back up on the best seller lists. Forman was an executive producer on the film, which enabled her to act as a connection between her readers and the filmmakers. While she didn't write the screenplay, she was allowed to see certain drafts of it. She was also able to advise the

THE STORY BEHIND THE STORIES

Almost all writers are inspired by the events around them. Many of these events and details become part of their stories. A good writer is also a good listener and picks stories from those around him or her. The truly interesting stories or the ones with niggling questions might end up woven together somewhere on the page.

Many of Forman's characters and books are inspired by real events. Her first novel, *Sisters in Sanity,* came about because of her fascination with adolescent boot camps after writing an article about them for *Seventeen*. She has said the accident in *If I Stay* was also inspired by true events. Her leading men are also often based on real men in her life. In numerous interviews she has talked about how the character of Adam shares much with her husband, Nick. In fact, he was even named Nick in early drafts, but her husband found that a little weird. The character of Willem in *Just One Day*, *Just One Year*, and *Just One Night* was based on the bartender who broke her heart when she lived in Amsterdam.

screenwriter about which scenes were most important to her fans.

SUCCESSFUL SEQUELS

With *If I Stay*, Forman created compelling characters. Readers wanted to know more about what happened to them following the events of the book. Forman was happy to oblige. In 2011, *Where She Went* was published. This book tells the story of Adam and Mia's next chapter. Mia is now a successful cellist studying her craft at the prestigious Juilliard School in New York City. Adam is also finding great success with his band, turning the tragic events that tore Mia and him apart in *If I Stay* into a best-selling album. Circumstances reunite the pair in New York, providing a compelling next chapter in their romantic saga. Unlike *If I Stay*, which is mostly told from Mia's point of view, *Where She Went* is told mostly from Adam's. This changing of viewpoints adds new insight to the story.

The Juillia

The Juilliard School in New York City remains one of the most prestigious performing arts schools in the country. The school enrolls around 850 students in the fields of dance, music, and theater.

In 2013, Forman published another book, this time not one about Adam and Mia. The book was called *Just One Day,* and the influences of Forman's own life in the story are clear to see. The novel follows a character named Allyson as she travels abroad for the first time on a teen trip. Much like Forman's earliest experiences abroad by herself, the teens journey to Europe. Allyson is a very organized and careful person. That all changes when she meets a Dutch actor, Willem, who invites her to throw caution to the wind and travel with him to Paris. Allyson, against her normally cautious character, agrees to go with him. So begins a wild and emotional twenty-four-hour adventure.

Before she wrote *Just One Day*, Forman took a research trip to Paris and roamed around the parts of the city that Allyson and Willem visit in order to get a sense of the area. She wanted to avoid all the clichés of love stories set in Paris.

Like *If I Stay* and *Where She Went, Just One Day* has a companion book told from a different point of view. The follow-up *Just One Year* is told from Willem's point of view. The book picks up right where *Just One Day* ended and details Willem's feelings about his day with Allyson. The second book is both a follow-up and another version of the original. It provides more insight into Willem and his own transformative journey. As a completion to the duet of novels, Forman wrote a short e-book that was released in 2014. The fifty-five-page novella *Just One Night* provides closure and an ending to Allyson's and Willem's story.

LIFE TODAY AND TOMORROW

These days, Forman continues to live with her family in Brooklyn, New York. Her husband, Nick, now works at ABC News and the pair take care of their two girls, Willa and Denbelle. Forman has said that balancing her life as a writer and work as a mother is sometimes difficult. She has to make sure to carve out enough time for each.

Forman writes almost every day. She describes her need for writing as almost an addiction. Even while she was on maternity leave and taking some time off from professional writing, she still made regular updates to her personal blog. Her brain created words and sentences, and she needed to put them down somewhere. In an interview with an online magazine called *The View From Here*, she described her

work space: she writes at her desk in the family living room. She listens to music sometimes when she writes, and often the music will help to inspire the writing. This was especially true of *If I Stay*, which had its own soundtrack. When writing this book, she frequently listened to the song "Falling Slowly" from the musical *Once.* The song both \made her sad and put her in the mood to compose.

At the same time, she believes it is important for a writer to not feel too isolated. She makes sure to leave her desk from time to time and engages with other people. She also actively communicates with her fan base. She blogs and responds to reader e-mail to feel more connected to the community.

Glen Hansard and Marketa Irglova, seen here, wrote the music for and starred in the movie *Once*. The song "Falling Slowly" from the film won the Academy Award for best song in 2007.

BECOMING A STRONG WRITER

Forman describes her greatest strength as a writer as also one of her greatest weaknesses. She considers herself something of a writing addict. It is hard for to her stop writing. Because of this, she starts many new projects whenever she is inspired. Unfortunately, some of these projects never see the light of day because she goes on to work on something else before finishing them. Sometimes finishing projects is not as easy as starting them. Luckily, with editors and publishers helping to guide her progress, she has been able to publish several novels in the last few years.

Part of being a writer is also being a voracious reader. To understand how to tell stories best and see different ways to mold language, it's valuable to read many books written by other people. Forman says she is inspired by other writers all the time. Much like traveling and talking to different people to absorb their stories, reading books takes her to other worlds. She can take in the language and be inspired to come up with her own ideas. She says she doesn't have a favorite author because she is impressed by so many different writers and their unique styles. She says she likes to read everything by one author, but then tires of one and moves onto

While Forman enjoys the work of many authors, she particularly admires Junot Diaz, seen here. She has described his style as "lyrical."

the next. She says she doesn't have much loyalty as a reader. She's glad her own fans are different than she is.

ON WRITING

In her personal blog, Gayle Forman shares tips on becoming a writer. As is the case with many lists of writing tips, one of her first tips is to take the advice with a grain of salt. There are no one-size-fits-all secret weapons in writing. What works for one writer might be terrible for another. With that first disclaimer about advice out of the way, her other suggestions are:

1. Write to your strengths. Don't worry about writing what everyone else will love; write what you love.
2. The best way to cure writer's block is to keep writing. Work on something else if you're truly at a sticking point, but whatever you do, don't stop writing.
3. Seek out the things that inspire you. If you get your best ideas on the bus, make sure always to have a pen and paper handy at the bus stop.
4. And finally...worry only about the writing, not trying to get published. One has to come before the other.

RECENT WRITINGS

When asked if she might write another novel about Adam and Mia to follow up *If I Stay* and *Where She Went*, Forman has said she won't. In a 2013 interview with the website Hypable, she said that she has been very grateful for fans' responses to the books and their excitement at the idea of another book. She feels like she has brought enough closure to their story, however, and left the characters where she wants them to be. Luckily, that doesn't mean she won't continue to write.

She has a number of recent works and doesn't show any sign of slowing down. In 2014, she released the e-book *Just One Night,* a novella-length work that offered a conclusion to the twin stories of *Just One Day* and *Just One Year.* In January 2015, she debuted another full novel. The book was titled *I Was Here*. It tackles tough issues as it examines the relationship between two childhood best friends—Meg and Cody—after one of them commits suicide. Like *Sisters in Sanity* many years before, the idea for this book came from an article she wrote for *Seventeen* on teen suicide back in her nonfiction days.

One of the girls Forman had written about for that story was a nineteen-year-old, Suzy Gonzales,

Forman isn't afraid to tackle serious emotional subjects in her novels. An unofficial tagline for her books that she sells on T-shirts on her website is "All. The. Feels."

who, according to her friends, had been a bright nonconformist, not so different from Forman herself. While interviewing Suzy's friends and family, Forman was left with the impression that she was learning about someone who would do incredible things, which made it that much more tragic that she couldn't interview Suzy as well because she had ended her own life. The image of Suzy and her story stayed with Forman, and she was the inspiration for the character of Meg. One detail about the story that Forman found particularly jarring was that Suzy had sent a time-delayed e-mail as a suicide note, so that by the time it arrived, she had already taken her own life. Forman couldn't help but wonder how it would feel to receive such an e-mail, so she made one take center stage in *I Was Here.* An important aspect that Forman hopes her readers take away from this book is that depression is a mental illness. She hopes to remove the stigma about mental illnesses so that people think of these illnesses no differently than physical illnesses.

If the subject of the book seems rather dark, it is not entirely out of character for Forman's books. She has definitely cemented herself as a talented writer of tragic and heart-wrenching stories. In an interview with the *Imagine Film List* blog, she described her philosophy on writing about heartbreak. To her, her books are not about heartbreak so much as redemption. The heartbreak comes in because in order to get to the redemptive ending, the characters must unfortunately go through some trials and tribulations first. According to Forman in an interview with *Bustle* in 2015, *I Was Here* is a suicide book that isn't about suicide. Ultimately it is about the surviving friend Cody's resilience as she comes to terms with the loss.

As part of the marketing for the release of *I Was Here*, Forman asked her followers on social media to post photos of themselves at places that were important to them or where they had had a major impact. They were instructed to tag the photos with the hashtag #IWasHere. As she explains: "#IWasHere is a rallying cry, recognizing the things you've done that have already had a ripple effect and made a mark on the world." She hoped by tagging the photos her readers would connect with the fact that they were constantly having an impact on the people around them.

Forman doesn't have much to offer on what she is writing currently; however, there's a good chance it won't be a laugh riot given her usual subject matter. In 2015, she revealed that she was working on two projects at the same time, enjoying taking a break from one when it gets hard to work on the other. Her readers and fans eagerly await these projects reaching completion.

A CHAMPION OF YA

Forman is a huge advocate for young adult (YA) literature. She believes it doesn't always get a fair shake, with some people thinking that it is not as legitimate as literature written for adults. She is a champion of young adult readers. She is continually impressed by her readership, and especially with the bloggers and social media savvy fans among them who share reviews of her books both good and bad. She loves when her writing can create a community around it, and she lurks on the blogs to learn more about it.

Forman believes the lines between young adult literature and adult literature have blurred over the years. Many adults pick up best-selling YA titles while many teens read novels that were originally written for adults. Naturally as a writer Forman is happy to accommodate an audience spanning decades in age and enjoys hearing from fans of all ages. In terms of the process of writing for YA, Forman described it in an interview with the blog *Motherlogue* as more streamlined than writing adult literature. Four pages of description can be cut down to one to focus more on the story. Another difference between YA books and books written for adults is that a lot of YA novels end on a hopeful note, if not always with a happy ending.

Forman champions many other authors in the young adult community. Here she is with Tonya Hurley at the book release party for Hurley's *Passionaries*.

While Forman is an admirer of her audience, her audience, as well as critics, are equally enamored with her work. She has won several awards for her writing. *If I Stay* won the National Atlantic Independent Booksellers Association Book of the Year Award in 2009. It also won an Indie Choice Honor Award and was a Quick Pick for Reluctant Young Adult Readers by the American Library Association. Its sequel, *Where She Went*, won the 2011 Goodreads Choice Award for Best Young Adult Fiction.

Gayle Forman has been lucky to have a successful writing career. She was able to discover a talent for storytelling and to indulge her love of traveling throughout her career. The choices she has made have helped shape her into the person and the writer she is today. Her stories are inspired by her own life and in many cases by the people she knows and loves or those she has met through her extensive travels. By seeing so much of the world and talking to so many people, Forman enriches her stories and creates strong characters who connect with readers. Her ability to connect with teen readers and her strong advocacy for young adult literature as its own powerful and important genre is clear to anyone who reads her tremendously popular books.

While she did not begin her novel-writing career until she was well into her thirties, Gayle Forman has already published several best sellers. Her readers and fans can only hope that she will publish many more wonderful novels in the years to come.

ON GAYLE FORMAN

Birth date: June 5, 1970
Birthplace: Los Angeles, California
Current home: Brooklyn, New York
First book: *You Can't Get There From Here: A Year on the Fringes of a Shrinking World* (2005)
First novel: *Sisters in Sanity* (2007)
Husband: Nick Tucker
Children: Daughters, Willa and Denbelle
Parents: Ruth and Lee Forman
College attended: University of Oregon
First job as a journalist: *Seventeen* magazine
Favorite country visited: India
Least favorite country visited: Tonga
Favorite color: Orange
First cat: Mischief, nicknamed "Missy"
Favorite band: Many, including the Velvet Underground, Sonic Youth, Pixies, Nirvana, the B-52s, the Go-Gos, the Magnetic Fields, Beat Happening, U2, the Waterboys, the Rolling Stones, Bikini Kill, Mumford & Sons, the Modern Lovers, the Clash, and Heavens to Betsy

ON GAYLE FORMAN'S WORK

Title: *Sisters in Sanity* (2007)
Plot: Brit Hemphill is sent by her father to a treatment center for wayward teens, but it turns out to be a sham filled with unqualified counselors doing more harm than good. She struggles to make friends, never sure whom to trust.

Title: *If I Stay* (2009)
Plot: Talented cellist Mia is in a horrible car accident that kills her family. While in a coma in the hospital, she has a choice: should she fight to stay alive or die with them? Complicating matters is her boyfriend, Adam, who desperately wants her to stay.
Awards: ALA Quick Pick for Reluctant Young Adult Readers; Milwaukee County Teen Book Award Nominee; 2009 NAIBA Book of the Year, Children's Literature; 2010 Indies Choice Young Adult Honor Award
Movie: Made into a movie starring Chloë Grace Moretz in 2014.

Title: *Where She Went* (2011)
Plot: Mia is now studying at Julliard while Adam is finding great success with his band back in Oregon. Fate brings them together in New York for one night as they question if they can change the past and have a future together.
Awards: Goodreads Choice Award, Best Young Adult Fiction; YALSA's 2012 Best Fiction for Young Adults List; YALSA's 2012 Teen's Top Ten; a *Publisher's Weekly* Best Children's Fiction Book of 2011

Title: *Just One Day* (2013)
Plot: Allyson is not used to taking chances. That is until she meets Willem while on a teen trip in Europe. Suddenly she finds herself throwing caution to the wind and traveling with him to Europe for one amazing day.
Awards: Goodreads Choice Award, Best Young Adult Fiction Nominee; YALSA's 2014 Best Fiction for Young Adults List

Title: *Just One Year* (2013)
Plot: After the events of *Just One Day*, Willem is lost without the girl he spent the day with in Paris. The story follows his months of traveling and questioning what his life would be like if he found her again.

Title: *Just One Night* (2014)

Plot: This novella provides a conclusion to the story of Willem and Allyson as fate brings them together again.

Title: *I Was Here* (2015)

Plot: Meg and Cody are best friends, until Meg suddenly takes her own life. A distraught Cody unravels the mystery of her friend's life and death while learning about friendship and her own life.

You Can't Get There from Here: A Year on the Fringes of a Shrinking World

"Armchair travelers will be sated by these smart, well-written tales."—*Publishers Weekly*

"A personal, engrossing description of a year of adventure and education."—*Library Journal*

Sisters in Sanity

"The place, characters, and story are well-drawn and believable. This suspenseful novel is full of heart."—*Children's Literature*

"Readers will care enough about the characters to want to know what happens to them."—*VOYA*

If I Stay

"A touching and emotional examination of love in all its forms ... and the choices, and sacrifices, we sometimes have to make for love. Incredibly sad, but life affirming and heart warming, everyone who has ever had to make a difficult choice involving things they love should read this book."—*The Bookbag*

"The stakes are poignantly conveyed through Mia's vivid memories of a rich, rewarding life."—*The Horn Book*

"Both brutal and beautiful, this thought-provoking story will stay with readers long after the last page is turned."—*School Library Journal*

Where She Went

"This book has compelling characters and a romance so deliciously fated that readers will be willing to suspend believability and embrace the growing mood of a fairy tale. Fans of the exceptional first novel won't be able to put this one down."— *School Library Journal*

"Forman tells an emotionally wrenching story that believably captures the mature depth and intensity possible in teenage love as well as the infinite ways that grief of all kinds permeates daily life."—*Booklist*

Just One Day

"Offering mystery, drama, and an evocative portrait of unrequited love, this open-ended novel will leave fans eagerly anticipating the companion story."—*Publishers Weekly*

"Reading like a teen version of Elizabeth Gilbert's *Eat, Pray, Love*, this tale of romance and mystery engages readers and will cause them to examine their definitions of love and self-identity."—*School Library Journal*

Just One Year

"An alluring story that pushes beyond the realm of
star-crossed romance."—*Publishers Weekly*

"As satisfying as both of these books are, readers are
going to wish for a third."—*Booklist*

I Was Here

"A haunting, elegiac tale about enduring and understanding loss."—*The Horn Book*

"An engrossing and provocative look at the devastat-
ing finality of suicide, survivor's guilt, the
complicated nature of responsibility and even
the role of the Internet in life-and-death
decisions."—*Kirkus*

"Forman...spin[s] heartbreak into [a mystery] that
remain[s] realistically, uncomfortably unsolved.
Readers requiring total resolution may want to
steer clear. But braver souls, teenagers and
adults alike, will be rewarded."—*The New York
Times Book Review*

1970 Gayle Forman is born in Los Angeles, California on June 5.

1991–1996 Forman lives in Eugene, Oregon, while going to college at the University of Oregon.

1997–2002 She works as a writer and editor at *Seventeen* magazine.

2002–2003 She travels the world with her husband, Nick.

2005 Her first book, *You Can't Get There From Here: A Year on the Fringes of a Shrinking World,* is published by Rodale on April 2.

2007 Her first novel, *Sisters in Sanity,* is released on September 1.

2009 *If I Stay* is published on April 2.

2010 She serves on a panel about young adult fiction at the Los Angeles Times Festival of Books on April 25.

2011 The follow-up to *If I Stay, Where She Went,* comes out on April 5. It is announced that *Where She Went* has won the Goodreads Choice Award for Young Adult Fiction for the year on December 6.

2013 *Just One Day* is published in January. *Just One Year* comes out in October.

2015 The book *I Was Here* is released on January 27.

GLOSSARY

ADAMANT Unshakable; unwilling to change one's mind.

ADVOCATE A supporter of a certain cause or policy.

ANCESTRY One's long-past relatives or ethnic descent.

ANTIMATERIALISTIC Not valuing physical things.

APARTHEID A government policy of racial segregation in South Africa that ended in 1994.

ASPIRATION A hope or plan for the future.

BOLLYWOOD The movie industry based in the Indian capital of Mumbai.

BURGEONING Quickly growing and improving.

CAPITALISM An economic system in which businesses and profits are controlled by the people instead of the government.

COMPILE To collect in one place.

DEMOGRAPHIC A target audience.

FORAY An advance on new territory.

FRAUGHT Stressed; undergoing anxiety.

GROSS To make money, especially referring to a film.

HOSTEL A cheap, efficient place for travelers to stay.

INCISIVE Having a sharp mind.

INCUBATOR A protected place where people can grow and mature.

INSTILL To establish an idea or attitude.

ITINERARY A plan, especially one for travel.

LONG-FORM In journalism, having a form that is a cross between a regular article and a novel.

NONCONFORMIST A person who follows his or her own path.

NOVELLA A piece of fiction shorter than a novel.

OFFICIATE To preside over a ceremony, such as a wedding.

PRACTITIONER A person following a certain profession.

PRECOCIOUS Having intelligence beyond one's years.

PUNK ROCK A loud and aggressive type of rock music developed in the late 1970s.

REDEMPTION Recovering from failure or sin.

SPASTIC In slang, awkward and clumsy.

STIGMA Disgrace or shame related to a certain idea or circumstance.

TRAJECTORY The direction something is traveling in.

VERACITY Accuracy; truth.

VORACIOUS Very eager.

Assembly on Literature for Adolescents
1111 W. Kenyon Road
Urbana, IL 61801
(217) 328-3870
Website: http://www.alan-ya.org
This organization, a part of the National Council for
    Teachers of English, promotes communication
    among those with an interest in YA literature. The
    organization sponsors numerous awards for
    writers of YA fiction.

Deb Shapiro & Co.
110 Riverside Drive, 1J
New York, NY 10024
(212) 496-5808
Website: http://www.debshapiroandcompany.com
This public relationships and marketing company has
    represented Gayle Forman and her books. They
    help advertise her books with targeted cam-
    paigns to make sure they find their market.

Gernert Company
136 East 57th Street, 18th Floor
New York, NY 10022
(212) 838-7777
Website: http://www.thegernertco.com
This literary agency represented several of Gayle
    Forman's books, including *Just One Day*.

Los Angeles Times Festival of Books
University of Southern California
University Park Campus
Los Angeles, CA 90089
Website: http://events.latimes.com/festivalofbooks
Begun in 1996, this festival is devoted to those who
write books and those who read them. Gayle
Forman spoke on a panel discussion on young
adult literature at the festival in 2010.

MediaBistro
770 Broadway, 15th Floor
New York, NY 10003
(212) 966-8984
Website: http://www.mediabistro.com
MediaBistro is a job site for freelancers and those in
creative industries, but it also provides résumé-
building courses, including writing classes.
Gayle Forman taught classes on travel writing
here until 2008.

Seventeen
300 W. 57th Street, 17th Floor
New York, NY 10019
Website: http://www.seventeen.com
This magazine was the first published in the United
States specifically targeting teen girls. A subsid-
iary of the Hearst Corporation, it is now the
largest monthly teen magazine. The magazine

offers internships for college credit to aspiring writers and editors.

Young Adult Library Services Association
50 E. Huron Street
Chicago, IL 60611
(800) 545-2433
Website: http://www.ala.org/yalsa
This division of the American Library Association (ALA) is devoted to expanding and strengthening library resources for teens and young adults ages twelve to eighteen.

WEBSITES

Because of the changing nature of Internet links, Rosen Publishing has developed an online list of websites related to the subject of this book. This site is updated regularly. Please use this link to access the list:

http://www.rosenlinks.com/AAA/Forman

Bailey, Diane. *Suzanne Collins* (All About the Author). New York, NY: Rosen Publishing, 2013.

Bell, Colin C. *On Their Own: A Story of Street Children in Thailand.* Bangkok, Thailand: BooksMango, 2014.

Brooks, Regina. *Writing Great Books for Young Adults: Everything You Need to Know from Crafting the Idea to Getting Published.* Naperville, IL: Sourcebooks, 2014.

Brown, Tracy. *Stephanie Meyer* (All About the Author). New York, NY: Rosen Publishing, 2013.

Deakin, Kathleen, and Laura A. Brown. *John Green: Teen Whisperer* (Studies in Young Adult Literature). Washington, DC: Rowman & Littlefield Publishers, 2015.

Dwyer, Rachel. *Bollywood's India: Hindi Cinema as a Guide to Contemporary India.* London, England: Reaktion Books Ltd., 2014.

Forman, Gayle. *If I Stay.* New York, NY: Penguin Books, 2009.

Forman, Gayle. *I Was Here.* New York, NY: Viking Books, 2015.

Forman, Gayle. *Just One Day.* New York, NY: Penguin Books, 2013.

Forman, Gayle. *You Can't Get There From Here: A Year on the Fringes of a Shrinking World.* New York, NY: Rodale, 2005.

Fountas, Irene. *Teaching with Fiction and Nonfiction Books.* Mankato, MN: Heinemann, 2012.

Furgang, Adam. *Rick Riordan* (All About the Author). New York, NY: Rosen Publishing, 2012.

Greenhaven Press. *Teen Suicide* (At Issue). San Diego, CA: Greenhaven Press, 2014.

Kole, Mary. *Writing Irresistible Kidlit: The Ultimate Guide to Crafting Fiction for Young Adult and Middle Grade Readers.* Ontario, Canada: Fraser Direct, 2012.

Martin, William Patrick. *A Lifetime of Fiction: The 500 Most Recommended Reads for Ages 2 to 102.* Lanham, MD: Rowman & Littlefield Publishers, 2014.

Mazer, Anne, and Ellen Potter. *Spilling Ink: A Young Writer's Handbook.* New York, NY: RB Flash Point/Roaring Brook Press, 2010.

McCoy, Mary. *Making Sense of Tonga.* La Jolla, CA: Mary McCoy, 2012.

Muchens, Juliet. *Get Started in Writing Young Adult Fiction.* New York, NY: Teach Yourself Books, 2015.

Potter, Ellen, and Anne Mazer. *Spilling Ink: A Young Writer's Handbook.* New York, NY: Roaring Brook Press, 2010.

Reber, Deborah. *In Their Shoes: Extraordinary Women Describe Their Amazing Careers.* New York, NY: Simon and Schuster, 2015.

Shorto, Russell. *Amsterdam: A History of the World's Most Liberal City.* New York, NY: Random House, 2013.

Weiss, Brad. *Street Dreams and Hip Hop Barbershops: Global Fantasy in Urban Tanzania.* Bloomington, IN: Indiana University Press, 2009.

Zhansasgimova, Dina. *Kazakhstan: The Essential Guide to Customs & Culture.* London, England: Kuperard, 2013.

Corbett, Sue. "Q & A with Gayle Forman." *Publishers Weekly*. April 30, 2009.

First Novels Club. "Interview with Gayle Forman." August 5, 2009. Retrieved March 10, 2015 (http://www.firstnovelsclub.com/2009/08/interview-with-gayle-forman.html).

Forman, Gale. "Biography." Retrieved March 3, 2015 (http://gayleforman.com/bio/).

Forman, Gayle. "Girls in Exile." *Seventeen*, September 2001. Retrieved March 3, 2015 (http://www.gayleforman.com/uploads/2007/08/girlsinexile.pdf).

Forman, Gayle. *If I Stay*. New York, NY: Penguin Books, 2009.

Forman, Gayle. *I Was Here*. New York, NY: Viking Books, 2015.

Forman, Gayle. *Just One Day*. New York, NY: Penguin Books, 2013.

Forman, Gayle. *Just One Year*. New York, NY: Penguin Books, 2014.

Forman, Gayle. *Sisters in Sanity*. New York, NY: Harper Teen, 2007.

Forman, Gayle. *Where She Went*. New York, NY: Penguin Books, 2011.

Forman, Gayle. "What the $%*!" March 22, 2010. Retrieved March 6, 2015 (http://gayleforman.com/blog/2010/03/22/what-the/).

Forman, Gayle. *You Can't Get There From Here: A Year on the Fringes of a Shrinking World.* New York, NY: Rodale, 2005.

Guardian. "Gayle Forman interview: 'Chloë Grace Moretz pushed out my mental image of Mia and became her.'" Retrieved March 6, 2015 (http://www.theguardian.com/childrens-books-site/2014/aug/27/gayle-forman-interview-if-i-stay-chloe-grace-moretz).

Goodreads Author Page. "Gayle Forman." Retrieved March 5, 2015 (http://www.goodreads.com/author/show/295178.Gayle_Forman).

IF List. "Exclusive: An Interview with Author Gayle Forman on Her Most Beautiful Male Lead and Upcoming Movies." February 26, 2015. Retrieved March 6, 2015 (http://blog.iflist.com/2015/02/26/exclusive-an-interview-with-author-gayle-for-man-on-her-most-beautiful-male-lead-and-upcoming-movies/).

Permanent Rain Press. "The Permanent Rain Press Interview with Gayle Forman." January 5, 2014. Retrieved March 5, 2015 (http://thepermanen-trainpress.com/post/72355576852).

View From Here. "Interview with Gayle Forman." Retrieved March 5, 2015 (http://www.viewfrom-heremagazine.com/2009/04/interview-with-gayle-forman-part-1-of-2.html).

White, Caitlyn. "Gayle Forman Talks About Her New Book 'I Was Here' And Why It's a Suicide Book That Isn't About Suicide." *Bustle*, January 28, 2015. Retrieved March 7, 2015 (http://www.bustle.com/articles/60028-gayle-forman-talks-about-her-new-book-i-was-here-and-why-its-a-suicide-book).

Whyte, Marama. "Author Interview: Gayle Forman on 'If I Stay' Movie Adaptation, Her Next Book, More." Hypable, June 5, 2013. Retrieved March 7, 2015 (http://www.hypable.com/gayle-forman-interview-if-i-stay-movie-just-one-year/).

INDEX

I

J

K

L

M

N

O

Y

Z

ABOUT THE AUTHOR

Susan Meyer is a writer of fiction and nonfiction and lives in Austin, Texas, with her husband, Sam. Like Gayle Forman, she is a great admirer of both travel and of young adult fiction.

PHOTO CREDITS